GEORGIA

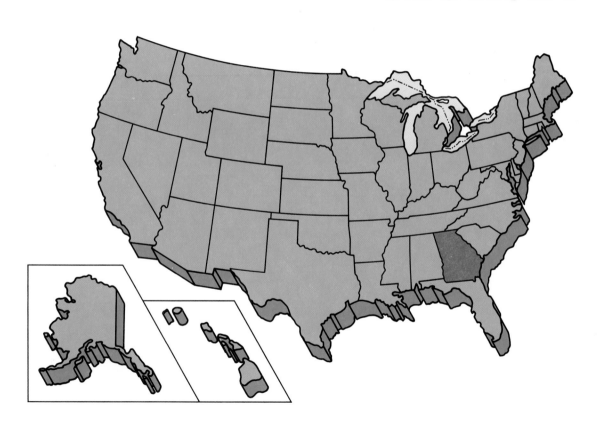

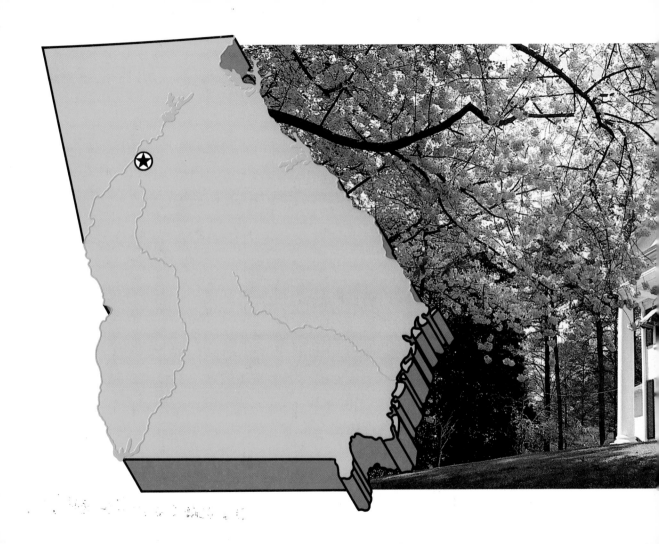

GEORGIA

Rita C. LaDoux

Lerner Publications Company

LIBRARY OF CONGRESS
CATALOGING-IN-PUBLICATION DATA
LaDoux, Rita.
    Georgia / Rita C. LaDoux.
      p. cm. — (Hello USA)
    Includes index.
    Summary: Introduces the geography, history, industries, people, and other highlights of Georgia.
    ISBN 0-8225-2703-0 (lib. bdg.)
    1. Georgia—Juvenile literature.
[1. Georgia.] I. Title. II. Series.
F286.3.L33 1991
975.8—dc20   90-38212
                    CIP
                    AC

Cover photograph courtesy of Georgia Department of Industry and Trade, Tourism Division.

The glossary that begins on page 68 gives definitions of words shown in **bold type** in the text.

 This book is printed on recycled paper.

CONTENTS

Did You Know . . . ?

☐ Eating fried chicken with a fork is against the law in Gainesville, Georgia, the Poultry Capital of the World.

☐ In 1985 the Atlanta Braves hosted the New York Mets in a game that made baseball history. The first pitch crossed the plate at 9:04 on the night of July 4th, but the game did not end until 3:55 the next morning—the latest a National League game has ever ended. The Mets won this 19-inning game by a score of 16 to 13.

❏ The first Coca-Cola was sold in Atlanta in 1886. A drugstore offered the beverage both as a soft drink and as a medicine!

❏ The first gold rush in the United States began in 1828 at Dahlonega, Georgia.

❏ Nearly half of the peanut butter eaten in the United States is made from peanuts grown in Georgia. Because Georgia's farmers produce more of these nuts than farmers in any other state, Georgia has earned the nickname the Goober State. (The word "goober" comes from *nguba*, an African word for peanut.)

7

Sand dunes drift across beaches on Georgia's Sea Islands.

A Trip
Around the State

Blackbeard the pirate once buried treasure on the Sea Islands off the coast of Georgia. Legends say that there are still riches hidden on these islands, also called the Golden Isles. Blackbeard's booty may never be found, but the land of Georgia also holds many treasures that are easy to uncover.

Seashell treasures wash up on shore.

9

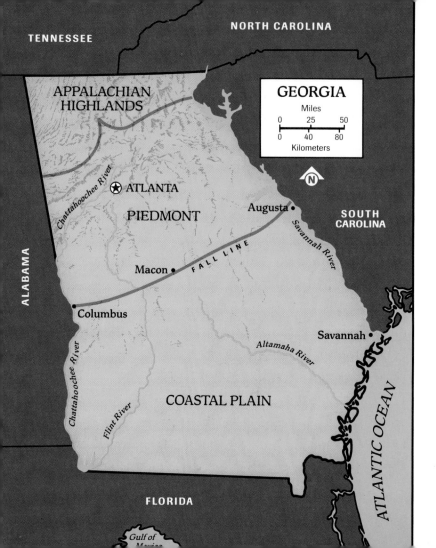

Georgia lies in the southeastern United States. Neighboring states are North Carolina, South Carolina, Tennessee, Alabama, and Florida. The Atlantic Ocean laps against Georgia's coast, which is 100 miles (161 kilometers) long. Georgia's Sea Islands protect the mainland from rough Atlantic waves.

Georgia can be divided into three geographic regions—the Appalachian Highlands, the Piedmont, and the Coastal Plain. The land, climate, plants, and animals are different in each area.

Georgia's Appalachian Highlands are part of the oldest mountain chain in North America. The entire chain stretches thousands of miles, from northern Georgia all the way into Canada. When they were young, these mountains had sharp, jagged peaks, but over millions of years, wind and rain have worn them down.

Mist shrouds the Blue Ridge Mountains in the Appalachian Highlands.

Water falling over dams at the Fall Line once spun wheels that turned millstones to grind grain.

The Piedmont region spans central Georgia. The Piedmont's rolling hills cover a **plateau** (high flat land) made of hard rock. Clay stains the soil of this area a rusty red. The southern boundary of the Piedmont is called the Fall Line. At this line, rivers form waterfalls as they tumble off the higher Piedmont Plateau and onto the lower land of the Coastal Plain—the southern region of the state.

Long ago, the Fall Line lay at the edge of a sea that flooded the Coastal Plain. Clay and sand settled to the bottom of this ancient ocean and later became the soils of the plain after the sea pulled back to its present shoreline. **Marshes** line the shore where the lowland meets the ocean.

The Okefenokee Swamp lies along the border between Georgia and Florida.

13

Fall colors highlight the shore of Lake Jasper in northern Georgia.

Many of Georgia's rivers have names given to them by the Native Americans, or Indians, who once lived in the area. Two of these rivers, the Savannah and the Altamaha, are the main waterways that flow southeast to the Atlantic Ocean. In western Georgia, the Chattahoochee and the Flint run south toward the Gulf of Mexico.

Humans have created the state's only large lakes by building dams to hold back rivers. People enjoy swimming and fishing in these lakes, but the main reason the rivers were dammed was to provide energy. The force of rushing water released from the dams turns large engines that produce electricity.

Georgia has many rainy days, especially in the summer. Fall is the driest season. The average yearly rainfall is 50 inches (127 centimeters). The Atlantic Ocean and the Gulf of Mexico send warm, moist air into the area. Hurricanes (tropical storms) often approach Georgia's shores.

The Piedmont and the Coastal Plain have mild winters, hot summers, and rainfall year-round. In the mountainous north, temperatures are lower than they are in southern and central Georgia.

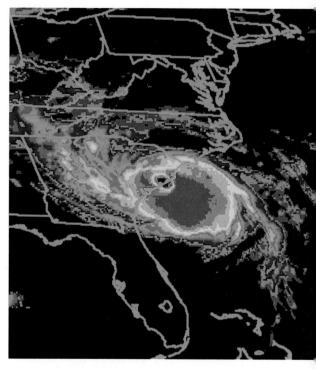

This picture taken by a weather satellite shows a hurricane striking the Atlantic coast. Strong winds and heavy rains whirl around the hurricane's eye, the dark area in the center.

Cypress trees arch over the almost still waters of the Okefenokee Swamp, also called the Land of the Trembling Earth. The islands in the swamp appear to tremble because they are not rooted in the ground.

The floating masses are made of decaying plant material and are covered with bushes and weeds. Alligators and snakes slither among the floating mounds.

Sugar maple and beech trees

An alligator's toothy grin welcomes campers at the Okefenokee Swamp.

Two black right whales, a mother and her calf, swim near the coast of Georgia. The calf is showing its white underside. Like all right whales, the mother can be identified by the unusual shape of her head.

grow in northern Georgia. Much of the southern half of the state is blanketed with pine and oak trees. Deer, black bears, foxes, and opossums roam Georgia's woodlands.

Fish, crabs, oysters, and shrimp use marshes on the Atlantic coast as nurseries for their young. Sea turtles lay their eggs on the Sea Islands' beaches. And within 5 to 10 miles (8 to 16 km) of Georgia's coast, black right whales—some of the world's rarest whales—give birth to their calves.

17

At the Ocmulgee National Monument, visitors can go inside an earthen lodge that was used by Indians 1,000 years ago.

Georgia's Story

Pirates, gold mines, and cotton plantations each play a part in Georgia's past. But the history of people in the area that is now Georgia begins long before pirates arrived in the 1700s. The story begins about 10,000 years ago, when Native Americans entered the region. Over time, many different groups of Indians have lived in the area.

Temple mound builders buried these marble statues in graves at Georgia's Etowah Mounds.

One group, known as the temple mound builders, settled in riverside villages. Craftspeople carved stone pipes and shell jewelry, and farmers raised beans, corn, and squash. These Indians built huge, flat-topped mounds for worshipping the sun and for burying their dead.

Around 1500, these Indians stopped building mounds. No one really knows what happened to the temple mound builders. They may have died from disease, or they may have been conquered by tribes moving into the area.

19

The Creek Indians became the most powerful tribe in the region about the same time that the mound builders disappeared. The Creeks built small villages along the rivers. Later, Cherokee Indians moved down from the north into Georgia's Appalachian Highlands.

In both Cherokee and Creek groups, women, children, and old men farmed. The younger men hunted deer, buffalo, and wild turkeys. The Cherokee and the Creeks were the two major Native American groups that lived in the area in 1540, the year that Hernando de Soto arrived in what is now Georgia.

De Soto was the first European to explore the region. He and his Spanish soldiers were searching for gold. They fought the Cherokee and Creek Indians and killed or captured many people. During and after de Soto's destructive visit, large numbers of Indians died from European diseases such as smallpox and measles, which they caught from the explorers.

In the 1500s, Spain and France each claimed the territory that is now Georgia. In the early 1600s, Britain also declared ownership of the region. Each country disagreed with the claims made by the others.

Blackbeard the Pirate

Many pirates raided ships along the Atlantic coast, but Blackbeard, from Britain, was one of the most bloodthirsty. He carried six guns, and when he had too much to drink he would even shoot his own men. Legends say that Blackbeard braided rope into his long hair. Then, to make himself look fierce, he lit the rope so that his face was surrounded by fire.

In 1716 Blackbeard raised his flag over the Sea Islands that are now part of Georgia. From bases on these islands, the ruthless British pirate and his rowdy men attacked ships to search for rum and treasure. In 1718 the British navy captured Blackbeard's boat and ended his piracy.

James Oglethorpe *(left)* was a member of the British Parliament and the founder of the colony of Georgia.

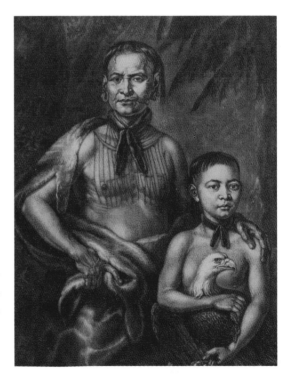

Tomochichi *(right)*, chief of the Yamacraw Indian tribe, became friends with Oglethorpe when the colonists arrived at the mouth of the Savannah River. The boy pictured with Tomochichi was his nephew Toonahowi.

The British strengthened their claim to the disputed land by making it a **colony.** As a colony, the territory would be settled by people who would be governed from Britain.

James Oglethorpe, a British leader, wanted the new colony to be a home for some of his country's needy citizens. He also wanted to help struggling people from all over Europe. He brought together a group of wealthy British people who agreed to help many of the travelers who had no money for the journey to North America.

On February 12, 1733, Oglethorpe and 35 families arrived in Georgia at the mouth of the Savannah River. Tomochichi, the chief of a small tribe called the Yamacraw Indians, helped the colonists build their first city, Savannah. The Creek Indians, who also lived nearby, made friends with the colonists and taught them how to fish and hunt. The new colony was named Georgia after George II, the king of Britain.

The leaders of Spain were very angry about the new British colony. In 1742 the Spanish attacked Georgia. In spite of being outnumbered, the colonists and their Indian friends defeated the Spanish in the Battle of Bloody Marsh. This was the last time Spain tried to take over the territory.

Posters like the one above announced slave auctions. Traders considered slaves property, not people. They separated families, selling mothers, fathers, and children to different buyers.

Georgia's early colonists did not use slaves (unpaid workers who are owned by other people). But beginning in 1749, shiploads of African people who had been captured in their homeland were brought to Georgia and traded for goods produced in the colony. Georgia's farmers forced their new slaves to plant and harvest rice.

In 1763 the British won the French and Indian War (a war fought over land in North America), and France gave up its claim to Georgia and other territories. For a short time, Britain's ownership of Georgia was unquestioned. But in the 1770s, some Georgians began to demand independence, or freedom, from the king's rule.

Georgians who wanted independence were called Whigs. Many others, known as Tories, wanted to remain loyal to Britain. The two groups often clashed.

People in all 13 of the British colonies also wanted independence. In 1775 the American Revolution began when those colonists took up arms to fight British troops. Georgians read about the war on the pages of the *Georgia Gazette,* the colony's first newspaper.

In March 1776, Georgia's rebels fought British soldiers for the first time. Four months later, three men from Georgia were among those who signed the Declaration of Independence—an official letter telling the king that all 13 colonies were breaking ties with Britain.

Georgia's first flag was designed in 1799. The version used since 1956 *(shown here)* combines the state seal and the battle flag of the Confederacy.

independence. In 1788 Georgia joined the Union as the fourth state.

Soon a new king—King Cotton—ruled Georgia. Cotton was usually grown on **plantations**, large farms that were worked by slaves. The white planters began looking for more land on which to plant cotton. By 1827 the state of Georgia and the U.S. government had forced the Creek Indians to sell their homeland.

The Revolution continued, and Georgia became a major battleground. Colonial soldiers forced the British out of Georgia in 1782, a year before the colonists won their

Eli Whitney and King Cotton

In the 1790s, Georgia's planters had a chance to become rich. Textile (cloth) mills in Britain needed more and more raw cotton. But the farmers had a problem.

The fluffy white fibers used to make cloth are tightly attached to a seed, much like hairs are attached to your head. The best way to remove the fibers had always been to pull them off by hand. This took a lot of time, and workers could clean only small amounts of cotton each day. Farmers could not keep up with the demand.

In 1793 Eli Whitney, a young teacher from Connecticut, visited Catherine Greene's plantation near Savannah. Greene asked Whitney to design a machine that would remove the cotton fibers from the seed. Within six months he had built his first cotton gin (short for engine). Whitney claimed that his machine could pick fibers off the seeds 50 times faster than a person could.

The original machine was fairly simple. The cotton boll (seed pod and its attached fibers) fell against a long, slotted plate that looked like a comb. Turning behind the plate was a cylinder, or tube, covered with spikes of wire. As the cylinder spun, the wires reached through the openings in the plate and grabbed pieces of cotton fiber.

Whitney had one last puzzle to solve. How could he get the cotton off the wires? Some people say that Greene suggested a brush would help. Whitney added a brush-covered cylinder to pull the fibers off the wire spikes, and his machine was complete.

The cotton gin was an immediate success. In the first 10 years alone, Georgia's production of cotton increased from 1,000 bales a year to 20,000 bales a year. Planters grew more and more cotton throughout the southern states. Eli Whitney's invention had crowned King Cotton.

The Cherokee were given no time to pack food or warm clothing for the 1,000-mile (1,610-km) march to Oklahoma.

Georgia promised its residents even more riches in 1828, when gold was discovered on Cherokee land. Fortune seekers rushed into the area to pan mountain streams for the precious metal.

Georgians, hungry for gold and more land, wanted the Cherokee territory. In the winter of 1838, the U.S. Army forced 14,000 Cherokee to march to the area that is now Oklahoma. Four thousand people died from disease and exposure to cold weather along the way, and the journey became known as the Trail of Tears.

The need for workers grew as planters turned more and more land into cotton fields. By 1860 over 460,000 slaves toiled in Georgia. Despite the large numbers of workers, only one out of every three farmers owned slaves. Most Georgians had small farms that they worked themselves.

Some people, especially those from the Northern states, believed that slavery was an unfair way to treat fellow human beings. But plantation owners saw slavery as a way to earn money. Good workers were so valuable that many Southern farmers had spent more money buying slaves than purchasing land. To make profits, cotton plantations depended on the labor of these unpaid workers.

Some rich plantation owners built mansions, but most cotton farmers lived in plain houses such as this one on the Jarrell Plantation.

FLAGS used in the CIVIL WAR

Confederate

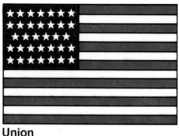

Union

Arguments between Northern and Southern states over slavery and other issues grew strong. In January 1861, Georgia and other Southern states decided to break away from the Union. They formed the Confederate States of America, a separate country in which slavery was allowed. The Civil War—the war between the North and South—broke out three months later.

In 1863 the South won the Battle of Chickamauga, the first major battle fought in Georgia. Losses were great for both sides in this fight. After two days of struggling, over 34,000 wounded or dead soldiers lay scattered across the battlefield.

Southern soldiers were the first Americans to make peanuts popular. When the rebels ran out of food, they ate the peanuts that farmers had grown to feed livestock.

Confederate and Union soldiers fought hand-to-hand in the Battle of Atlanta. By the end of the Civil War, nearly 125,000 Georgians had died in the fighting.

General William Tecumseh Sherman and his Northern troops surrounded Atlanta in the summer of 1864. When the city ran out of food and ammunition, Confederate soldiers abandoned Atlanta.

Next, during Sherman's March to the Sea, soldiers fighting for the North raided farms and destroyed the factories, railroads, and bridges lying between Atlanta and Savannah. Confederate soldiers fighting north of this line were cut off from their supplies of food and weapons. The Civil War continued until April 1865, when the South surrendered to the North.

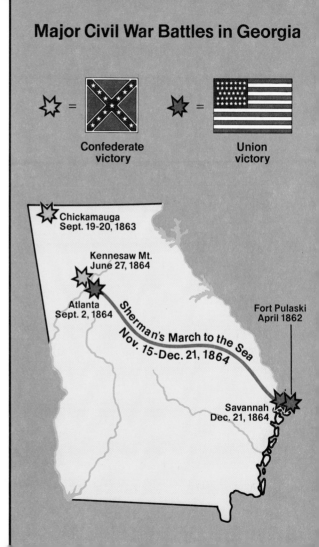

Major Civil War Battles in Georgia

☆ = Confederate victory

★ = Union victory

Chickamauga
Sept. 19-20, 1863

Kennesaw Mt.
June 27, 1864

Atlanta
Sept. 2, 1864

Sherman's March to the Sea
Nov. 15-Dec. 21, 1864

Fort Pulaski
April 1862

Savannah
Dec. 21, 1864

Atlantans destroyed their railroad station so that Union troops could not use it.

The war left Georgia scarred and broken. Farms and homes had been ruined, and many people had died. The U.S. government had freed the slaves. This meant that Southern plantation owners lost not only their unpaid laborers but also the money they had spent to buy the slaves. Some farms could no longer afford to operate.

Freedom from slavery did not change the lives of most black workers. Few of them had been allowed to get any education or to learn skills other than farm labor. So, although some former slaves moved to cities, many continued to work in the fields.

Workers weighed the day's cotton harvest.

After the war, the U.S. government ruled Georgia during a time called **Reconstruction** (rebuilding). While some Georgians began to rebuild railroads and start new industries, others reorganized the state government. In 1870 elected officials approved a law that gave black men the right to vote (earlier, only white men had been allowed to vote), and Georgia was able to rejoin the United States.

For several decades after Reconstruction, most Georgians still worked on farms growing cotton. Then disaster struck in the 1920s. Beetles called boll weevils gnawed their way through the cotton fields. Many farmers lost their entire crop and had to abandon their land.

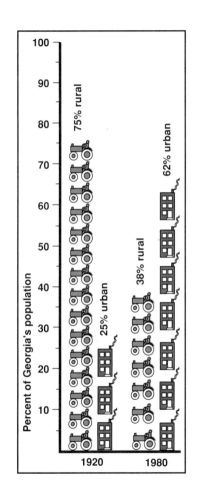

Between 1920 and 1980, many Georgians moved from the country to the city. By 1960 more Georgians lived in cities than in rural areas.

During World War II (1939–1945), many Georgians who lived in cities made supplies for the war. At the Bell Bomber Plant, men and women worked together to build airplanes.

Some civil rights demonstrations ended in violence, but the Reverend Martin Luther King, Jr., a native of Atlanta, tried to lead peaceful marches.

By this time, white politicians had found ways to keep African Americans from voting. Black men who wanted to register to vote had to take reading and writing tests. The people who graded the tests made sure that no black man—no matter how educated he was— would pass the test.

Black people also did not have the same **civil rights** (personal freedoms) as white people. For example, blacks could not go to the schools or restaurants that were reserved for whites. In the 1950s and 1960s, leaders organized marches throughout the southern states. These people demanded full civil and voting rights for black people.

King's speeches inspired people to demand their rights as American citizens. One important issue was the right to an equal education. In 1961 black leaders and white leaders worked together to help black students attend the same public schools as white students.

Timeline:

- 10,000 B.C. — Native Americans move into the area that is now Georgia
- A.D. 1540 — Spanish explorer Hernando de Soto passes through the region
- 1733 — James Oglethorpe leads British colonists to Savannah
- 1749 — First slaveships arrive in Georgia
- 1788 — Georgia becomes the fourth state to join the Union
- 1838 — Cherokees march to Oklahoma on the Trail of Tears

Since the civil rights marches, many Georgians have worked to give equal opportunities to everyone in the state. In 1973 Maynard Jackson, Jr., became the first African American to be elected mayor of Atlanta.

Another Georgian, Jimmy Carter, became a well-known politician in the 1970s. While he was governor of Georgia, Carter better organized the state government. He also worked to improve relationships between blacks and whites.

40

| 1861 | 1920 | 1961 | 1973 | 1977 |

Georgia joins the Confederate States of America; Civil War (1861–1865) begins

Boll weevils destroy Georgia's cotton crop

Atlanta public schools allow black students and white students in the same classrooms

Maynard Jackson, Jr., is elected mayor of Atlanta

Jimmy Carter becomes the 39th president of the United States

In 1976 Jimmy Carter was elected president of the United States. He served for four years.

The history of Georgia is made up of the stories of many people—Indian farmers, colonial planters, Confederate soldiers, civil rights marchers. Together, these people have given Georgia a rich past and a promising future.

41

Living and Working in Georgia

Georgia earned one of its nick-names, the Empire State of the South, because the state is the southern center for many big U.S. companies. Thriving businesses—both large and small—provide jobs for many Georgians. In recent years, people from throughout the United States have moved to Georgia to find employment (work) in the state's growing businesses.

Most of the big companies are located in Georgia's major cities. The growth of these cities follows the history of the cotton industry. By the early 1800s, Savannah had become a major port for shipping cotton to Britain. Now, workers at the modern port of Savannah load products for shipment all over the world.

Trucks and trains carry the goods made in Augusta, Columbus, and Macon to buyers across the country. But in the 1800s, these cities were bustling river ports. They were all located on the Fall Line, the farthest point upriver that cotton-carrying boats could travel. Over time these ports developed into major cities.

Atlanta is the capital and largest city of Georgia. It began as a post office at the last stop for trains traveling on the Western and Atlantic Railroad. Trains leaving Atlanta once carried cotton to textile mills in the northern states. Today, Atlanta is the major center in the southeastern United States for trade, transportation, and manufacturing. Almost half of all Georgians live in the Atlanta area.

City workers take their lunch break in Atlanta's Woodruff Park.

Between 1980 and 1990, the population of Georgia increased by about 1.2 million people (22 percent). In 1990, one out of every five people was a new resident. By the early 1990s, more than 6.6 million people lived in Georgia.

Most Georgians were born in the United States. About three-fourths of the people have ancestors from

Europe, and one-fourth have ancestors from Africa. Small numbers of the population are Native American, Asian, or Hispanic (of Spanish origin).

The history of Georgia—from Native American life to British colonial times to Civil War battles—is told at museums and historic sites throughout the state. Art museums, symphony orchestras, operas, theater, and dance draw audiences in many of Georgia's larger cities. And the voices of Georgia, from Appalachian fiddles to gospel choirs, sing out at festivals throughout the state.

A model of a dinosaur delights visitors at Fernbank Science Center.

45

Hairy Dawg leads cheers at the
University of Georgia's games *(left)*.
The Atlanta Falcons *(center)* and
Braves *(right)* attract many fans.

Sports fans find many exciting activities in Georgia. Atlanta is the home base for three professional athletic teams. The Braves score homeruns slugging baseballs, the Hawks make points slam-dunking basketballs, and the Falcons rack up yardage passing footballs. Also, professional golfers dream of winning the Masters Golf Tournament, a world-class competition held every year in Augusta.

The state's year-round mild climate makes it an outdoor paradise. Many Georgians find time to enjoy hiking, swimming, fishing, and hunting. Other people join cheering crowds at motorcycle and car races.

Cars race to the finish at Road Atlanta.

Although once king of Georgia, cotton is no longer the state's most important product. Over half of Georgia's workers do not make any products. Instead, they hold service jobs. People in service jobs help other people or businesses. They may work as salespeople, bankers, teachers, or tour guides.

One out of five Georgians earn their living from manufacturing. Textiles are the major manufactured product, and the state's most important textile is carpet.

Food products are also processed in Georgia. Some workers tend machines that crush peanuts and make peanut butter. Others pack fruits, vegetables, or seafood.

The world's largest drive-in, the Varsity, has been serving burgers in Atlanta since 1928.

Students and teachers learn about the natural world at environmental learning centers.

Many people work in plants that produce chemicals for farms and industries. Other employees work in factories that manufacture paint, medicine, or soap. Georgia's mechanics build airplanes, boats, and bodies for cars and trucks.

Foresters plant millions of fast-growing pine trees in southern Georgia each year. After just 20 years, these softwood trees are cut and milled into paper and paperboard. Some workers tap pine trees for sap that is made into turpentine (a paint thinner). Others use chemicals to break down wood into fibers that are used to make some types of plastic. And carpenters craft furniture from northern Georgia's hardwood trees.

Georgia's peaches are a summer treat.

You might think of peaches when you think of Georgia because it is sometimes called the Peach State. Many different kinds of this sweet fruit are harvested in Georgia's north central valleys. The state's watermelon fields and apple orchards also produce juicy fruits.

It's hard to decide whether the chicken or the egg comes first in Georgia because the state is a leading producer of both. Farmers sell about 2 million chickens and 12 million eggs every day. Other farmers raise pigs, dairy cows, and beef cattle.

Students inspect cotton during their school's annual Farm Day *(left)*. Peanut farmer and former president Jimmy Carter checks to see if his goobers are ripe *(below)*.

Georgia grows more **goobers,** or peanuts, than any other state. Other crops from Georgia include sweet potatoes, pecans, tobacco, corn, soybeans, hay, oats, and wheat. Some farmers still plant cotton, but now out of every one hundred dollars earned in the state cotton brings in only one cent!

51

The clay soils of Georgia provide a source of income for miners. Kaolin, a chalky white clay mined near the Fall Line, is used to make a fine china and to give paper a shiny finish. In Georgia's Piedmont and Appalachian Highland regions, workers cut slabs of granite, marble, and limestone for use in construction.

Along the Atlantic coast, fishing boats bring in catches of shrimp. Crabs, oysters, and shad make up most of the rest of the fishing harvest.

Georgia is not only a good place to live and work, it is also a great place to visit. With its beautiful coastal waters, scenic mountains, and mysterious swamplands, Georgia's natural beauty welcomes travelers. Add in the historical exhibits, sporting events, and entertainment, and you will know why every year over 20 million tourists visit Georgia.

Lasers and fireworks light up Stone Mountain. On the mountain in the background is a huge carving of three Confederate heroes—Jefferson Davis, Robert E. Lee, and Thomas "Stonewall" Jackson.

Protecting the Environment

The population of Georgia is growing quickly. Every year, workers clear forests to make room for more cropland, houses, and businesses. When people change their environment, they risk destroying the habitats of native plants and animals.

Georgia's state tree, the live oak, is one type of tree that provides rich habitats for a variety of animals and plants. Found throughout the Coastal Plain, these oak trees may live for hundreds of years. They have green leaves all

The live oak standing in Thomasville, Georgia, measures 68 feet (21 m) high and 162 feet (49 m) wide.

year round. Wild grapevines twine around the trunks and lower limbs of the oaks, and feathery Spanish moss hangs on the trees' higher branches.

Squirrels and songbirds chase through the oak trees, while bobcats crawl along the low branches.

During the day, moss and leaves hide sleeping brown bats, great horned owls, and flying squirrels. Each fall, black bears, deer, wild turkeys, and alligator snapping turtles feast on grapes from the vines and on acorns that fall from the trees.

People enjoy live oaks because of their beauty and the shade they provide. Some landowners, however, clear the trees to make room for new buildings or more crops. Felling just one live oak causes its numerous residents to lose their home. Cutting down these trees throughout the Coastal Plain robs large numbers of plants and animals of their habitats. And the live oak is only one of the many habitats that people destroy.

Some kinds of plants and animals are specialists. They can find their food and shelter in only a few places. When their habitat is changed, specialists are the most likely to become endangered species. Plants and animals become endangered when so few of them

The green pitcher plant eats insects that fall into its petal trap.

Loggerhead sea turtles lay eggs at night on the Sea Islands' beaches. This turtle is being tagged so that scientists will know if it returns another year.

are living that they could soon become extinct. This means they might die out completely.

The Georgia Department of Natural Resources (DNR) makes lists and maps of places where endangered species live. Georgians can help the DNR create these maps by reporting any unusual plants or animals they find. Builders who are concerned about wildlife use the DNR maps when choosing construction sites. They can plan to clear land and place buildings so that the special habitats are not harmed.

Bullfrogs spend most of their life in or near water.

Some Georgians are protecting the environment in their own backyards. They grow trees and plants that will make good living areas for their favorite kinds of animals.

For example, people who like lizards and frogs—or herps as these cold-blooded animals are called— create special gardens as homes for the creatures. During the day, shrubs offer damp hiding places for toads. Small ponds give toads and frogs a place to lay eggs, and large ponds provide a home for turtles. Gardeners who like lizards can add log piles or stone fences.

Bird-watchers can design and plant their backyards to draw in some feathered friends. Apple trees attract waxwings and warblers. Goldfinches and cardinals visit feeders full of sunflower seeds. And colorful flowering plants will draw in not only hummingbirds but also butterflies.

Raccoons make their homes both in wild areas and near people.

Whether the gardens are for herps, birds, or butterflies, many types of wildlife visit backyard habitats. At a time when natural habitats are being lost, these gardens can provide food and shelter for many animals. By building wildlife gardens and by indentifying and saving habitats, Georgians are helping to protect the environment in which they and other animals live.

**The endangered
Florida cougar needs
a forested home.**

Georgia's Famous People

◀ **KIM BASINGER**

Kim Basinger (born 1953) is from Athens, Georgia. She has starred in several motion pictures, including *The Natural*, *Blind Date*, and *Batman*. In 1989, Basinger bought the town of Braselton, Georgia. She plans to turn the town into a location for shooting movies.

Oliver Hardy (1892–1957) was born in Atlanta. A comedian, Oliver Hardy teamed up with Stan Laurel in 1926. Together, Laurel and Hardy made over 200 slapstick movies.

OLIVER HARDY ▶

TY COBB ▶

ATHLETES

Tyrus ("Ty") Cobb (1886–1961) was born near Homer, Georgia. Ty Cobb, the "Georgia Peach," was one of the all-time greatest baseball players. As a Detroit Tiger from 1905 to 1926, he won 12 American League batting titles and held the major league hitting record until 1985.

John ("Jackie") Robinson (1919–1972), a native of Cairo, Georgia, was the first black man to play for a major league baseball team. He started his career with the Kansas City Monarchs, a team in the Negro American League, and in 1947 joined the all-white Brooklyn Dodgers. He received the National League's Most Valuable Player award in 1949.

◀ **JACKIE ROBINSON** *(left)*

Wyomia Tyus Tillman (born 1945) became famous as an outstanding track athlete. Tyus, from Griffin, Georgia, won a gold medal for the 100-meter dash at the 1964 Olympic Games.

In 1968, she won another Olympic gold medal by running the 100-meter dash in just 11 seconds.

BUSINESS LEADERS & SCIENTISTS

Alonzo Herndon (1858–1927) was born a slave on a plantation near Social Circle, Georgia. After the Civil War, Herndon moved to Atlanta, where he opened a number of barbershops and became a wealthy man. In 1905 he founded the Atlanta Life Insurance Company. His company is now one of the largest black-owned businesses in the United States.

Crawford Williamson Long (1815–1878), who was born in Danielsville, Georgia, was the first physician to use ether (a chemical) as a painkiller during surgery. Long introduced the painkiller in 1842, when he gave it to a patient before removing a tumor from the patient's neck.

▲ ALONZO HERNDON

JULIETTE ► GORDON LOW

◀ SEQUOYA

EDUCATORS & YOUTH LEADERS

Juliette Gordon Low (1860–1927) lived in Savannah, Georgia, where she started the Girl Scouts of America in 1912. Her Savannah home is now the national headquarters for the organization.

Sequoya (George Gist) (1760?–1843) developed the first alphabet for an American Indian language. His symbols stood for sounds in Cherokee. Sequoya's alphabet was used in the *Cherokee Phoenix*, the first Indian newspaper, which was published at New Echota, Georgia, in 1828.

63

LEADERS

Martin Luther King, Jr. (1929–1968), a leader of the civil rights movement, was born in Atlanta. A Baptist minister, he worked to make life better for black people. In 1964 King won the Nobel Peace Prize. He was the youngest person ever to win this award.

John Ross (1790–1866) led his people, the Cherokee, in the struggle to keep their homeland in Georgia and neighboring states. In 1838 the U.S. Army forced Ross and his followers to march to land that is now in Oklahoma. Ross was elected chief of the Cherokee Nation in Oklahoma in 1839.

▲ MARTIN LUTHER KING, JR.

▼ RAY CHARLES

▲ GLADYS KNIGHT

MUSICIANS

Ray Charles (born 1930) is from Albany, Georgia. A singer and songwriter, Charles has won 10 Grammy Awards for his music. He sings in the movie *The Blues Brothers*. Charles was the first person to sing the new state song, "Georgia on My Mind," to the state legislature.

Amy Grant (born 1961) sings Christian rock music to audiences across the country. Grant, who is from Augusta, Georgia, has cut a number of albums, including *Age to Age*, which sold over one million copies.

Gladys Knight (born 1944) started singing in gospel choirs and talent contests in her hometown, Atlanta. At the age of eight, she formed a singing group with members of her family. That group, the Pips, has sung with Knight since 1952. Her well-known songs include "Operator," "Midnight Train to Georgia," and "I Heard It through the Grapevine."

◄ JIMMY CARTER

ALEXANDER STEPHENS ▶

James ("Jimmy") Carter, Jr. (born 1924), the 39th president of the United States, grew up on a peanut farm in Plains, Georgia. Carter was elected governor of Georgia in 1971. He served as president of the United States from 1977 to 1981. He now works on international issues at the Carter Center in Atlanta.

Alexander Hamilton Stephens (1812–1883) represented Georgia in the U.S. House of Representatives from 1843 to 1859. He was originally against having the South separate from the Union, but he eventually became vice-president of the Confederacy. After the Civil War, Stephens again served as a representative and later was elected governor of Georgia.

Andrew Jackson Young, Jr. (born 1932), was an assistant to Martin Luther King, Jr. In 1972 Young was elected to the U.S. House of Representatives. He was the first black representative from Georgia since the Reconstruction period. Young served as mayor of Atlanta from 1982 to 1990. He ran for the office of governor of Georgia in 1990.

WRITERS

Margaret Mitchell (1900–1949), who was born in Atlanta, wrote *Gone with the Wind*. Her only novel, it tells the story of Southerners during the Civil War. The book has sold over eight million copies and was made into a movie in 1939.

Alice Walker (born 1944), from Eatonton, Georgia, began writing stories and poems when she was eight years old. Her novel *The Color Purple* was made into an award-winning movie.

▲ ALICE WALKER

MARGARET MITCHELL ▶

65

Facts-at-a-Glance

Nicknames: Empire State of the South,
Peach State, Goober State
Song: "Georgia on My Mind"
Motto: Wisdom, Justice, Moderation
Tree: live oak
Flower: Cherokee rose
Bird: brown thrasher
Fossil: shark's tooth

Population: 6,663,000 (1990 estimate)
Rank in population, nationwide: 11th
Area: 58,910 sq mi (152,576 sq km)
Rank in area, nationwide: 21st
Date and ranking of statehood:
January 2, 1788, the 4th state
Capital: Atlanta
Major cities (and populations*):
Atlanta (421,910), Columbus (180,180), Savannah
(146,800), Macon (118,420), Albany (84,950),
Augusta (45,440)
U.S. senators: 2
U.S. representatives: 10
Electoral votes: 12

*1986 estimates

Places to visit: Stone Mountain near Atlanta,
Dahlonega Gold Museum, Okefenokee Swamp in
southeastern Georgia, Etowah Mounds near
Cartersville, Callaway Gardens near Pine Mountain

Annual events: St. Patrick's Day Festival in Savannah (March), Late Model Stock Car Race in Atlanta
(March), Spring Country Music Festival in Hiawas-
see (May), Watermelon Festival in Cordele (July),
Gold Rush Days in Dahlonega (Oct.)

66

| **Average January temperature:** 47° F (8° C) | **Average July temperature:** 80° F (27° C) |

Natural resources: forests, fertile soil, plentiful water, granite, marble, gold, kaolin, talc, soapstone, mica, limestone, sand, gravel

Agricultural products: chickens, peanuts, beef cattle, eggs, milk, tobacco, soybeans, corn, cotton, pecans, wheat, turkeys, peaches, hay

Manufactured goods: carpet, cotton cloth, clothing, chemicals, food products, paper products, lumber, furniture, turpentine, airplanes, car and truck bodies, machinery

ENDANGERED SPECIES
Mammals—black right whale, Florida panther, eastern cougar, gray bat, West Indian manatee
Birds—Kirtland's warbler, peregrine falcon, bald eagle, wood stork, eastern brown pelican
Reptiles—leatherneck turtle, hawksbill turtle, Atlantic ridley turtle
Fish—shortnose sturgeon, amber darter, Conasauga logperch, southern cave fish
Plants—hairy rattleweed, three-tooth cinquefoil, Hirst panic grass, green pitcher plant, false pimpernel, Curtiss loosestrife, persistent trillium

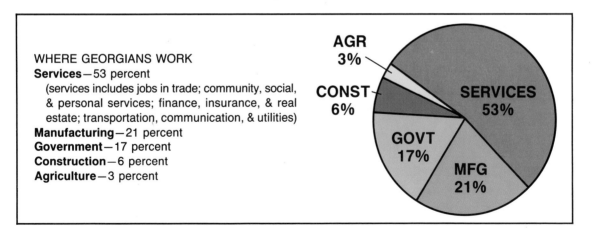

WHERE GEORGIANS WORK
Services—53 percent
  (services includes jobs in trade; community, social, & personal services; finance, insurance, & real estate; transportation, communication, & utilities)
Manufacturing—21 percent
Government—17 percent
Construction—6 percent
Agriculture—3 percent

67

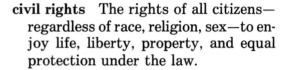

PRONUNCIATION GUIDE

Altamaha   (AWL-tuh-muh-haw)

Appalachian   (ap-uh-LAY-chuhn)

Augusta   (aw-GUH-stuh)

Chattahoochee   (chat-uh-HOO-chee)

Chickamauga   (chick-uh-MAW-guh)

Confederate   (cuhn-FEHD-uh-ruht)

Macon   (MAY-kuhn)

Oglethorpe   (OH-guhl-thorp)

Okefenokee   (oh-kuh-fuh-NOH-kee)

Piedmont   (PEED-mahnt)

Reconstruction
   (ree-kuhn-STRUHK-shuhn)

Savannah   (suh-VAN-uh)

Tomochichi   (toh-moh-CHEE-chee)

civil rights   The rights of all citizens—regardless of race, religion, sex—to enjoy life, liberty, property, and equal protection under the law.

colony   A territory ruled by a country some distance away.

goober   A word used primarily in the South to mean peanut. Goober comes from the African word *nguba*.

marsh   A spongy wetland soaked with water for long periods of time. Marshes are usually treeless; grasses are the main kind of vegetation.

plantation   A large estate, usually in a warm climate, on which crops are grown by workers who live on the estate. In the past, plantation owners often used slave labor.

plateau A large, relatively flat area that stands above the surrounding land.

Reconstruction The period from 1865 to 1877 during which the U.S. government brought the Southern states back into the Union after the Civil War. Before rejoining the Union, the Southern states had to pass laws allowing black men to vote. Places destroyed in the war were rebuilt and industries were developed.

Index ▰▰▰▰▰▰▰▰▰▰▰▰▰▰▰▰▰▰▰▰▰▰